は ハ ha	ひ ヒ hi	ふ フ fu	へ ヘ he	ほ ホ ho
ま マ ma	み ミ mi	む ム mu	め メ me	も モ mo
や ヤ ya		ゆ ユ yu		よ ヨ yo
ら ラ ra	り リ ri	る ル ru	れ レ re	ろ ロ ro
わ ワ wa				を ヲ o
ん ン n				

ば バ ba	び ビ bi	ぶ ブ bu	べ ベ be	ぼ ボ bo
ぱ パ pa	ぴ ピ pi	ぷ プ pu	ぺ ペ pe	ぽ ポ po

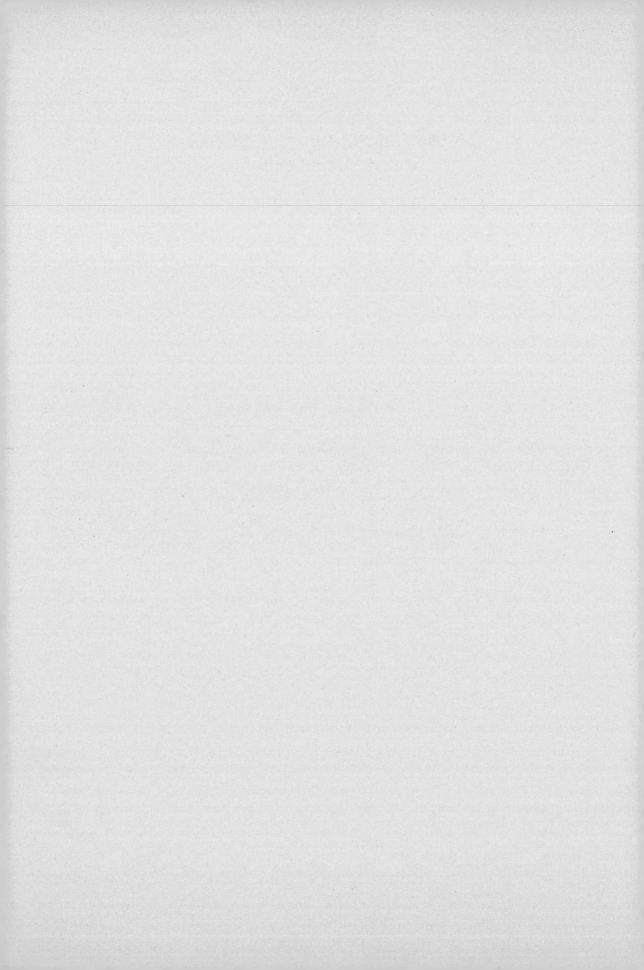

JAPANESE FOR BUSY PEOPLE
Kana Workbook

JAPANESE FOR BUSY PEOPLE

Kana Workbook

Association for Japanese-Language Teaching

KODANSHA INTERNATIONAL
Tokyo · New York · London

Acknowledgments

The book was compiled by four AJALT teachers:
Mss. Kyoko Ishikure, Miyako Iwami,
Satoko Mizoguchi, and Junko Shinada.
They were assisted by Ms. Miho Shimada.

Note: This book was previously published as *Kana for Busy People*.

The Authors: The Association for Japanese-Language Teaching (AJALT) was recognized as a nonprofit organization by the Ministry of Education in 1977. It was established to meet the practical needs of people who are not necessarily specialists on Japan but who wish to communicate effectively in Japanese. In 1992 the Association was awarded the Japan Foundation Special Prize.

The Association maintains a web site on the Internet at www.ajalt.org and can be contacted over the Internet via info@ajalt.org by teachers and students who have questions about this textbook or any of the Association's other publications.

Distributed in the United States by Kodansha America, Inc., 575 Lexington Avenue, New York, New York 10022, and in the United Kingdom and continental Europe by Kodansha Europe Ltd., 95 Aldwych, London WC2B 4JF.

Published by Kodansha International Ltd., 17-14 Otowa 1-chome, Bunkyo-ku, Tokyo 112-8652, and Kodansha America, Inc.

First edition, 1996
02 03 04 05 06 07 08 09 10   15 14 13 12 11 10 9 8 7

www.thejapanpage.com

CONTENTS

INTRODUCTION

It is the hopeful aim of the authors of this book to help students to master *kana*—both *hiragana* and *katakana*—much more easily and quickly than ever before. It is our further hope that our readers will consist not only of those whose native tongue is English, but also students of non-English-speaking countries who don't have workbooks such as this available in their mother tongue but who are conversant with English.

The text for the exercises found herein is based on *Japanese for Busy People*, volume 1 (JBP1), published by Kodansha International Ltd. To be more precise, the vocabulary and sentence structure borrow from lessons 1 through 10 and are introduced here in much the same order. Thus, while learning to read and write *kana*, the student will at the same time acquire vocabulary and become familiar with sentence structure. Once having finished *Kana Workbook*, the student should be able to read at the level of JBP1's Lesson 11, "Reading Review."

An Overview of the Book

Before embarking on the workbook itself, the student may find it worthwhile to get a general notion of its contents. That is what the remainder of the Introduction is devoted to. Note, first of all, however, that there is a *kana* table on the inside of the front cover, showing all the *hiragana* and *katakana* covered in this book, along with the appropriate romanization.

HIRAGANA 1
- The pronunciation of *hiragana* using the *kana* table

  Here you will listen carefully to the pronunciation of each *hiragana* syllable on the tape while studying the table. You should do this until both pronunciation and chart become virtually second nature.
- Coming to grips with the forms of *hiragana*

  The exercises in this section will give you a good visual sense of the formal features of *hiragana*.
- Writing the basic syllables

  After becoming familiar with how *hiragana* appear to the eye, here you will practice writing the basic syllables. The exercises are designed to help you to reproduce *hiragana* shapes as accurately as possible.
- Writing words

  First read the *hiragana* while concealing the romanization. Then practice writing the

hiragana while concealing the models. After some practice, try writing while listening to the tape rather than relying on the romanization in the book.
- Reading and writing modified syllables (*yō-on*), long vowels (*chō-on*), and double consonants (*soku-on*)

    The exercises here follow much the same pattern as those for the basic syllables above.

HIRAGANA 2

- Reading and writing sentences

    Through the reading and writing exercises in this section you will learn particle usage and sentence structure at the introductory level. Lesson 3 of JBP1 should be completed before tackling this part of the book.

    In Lessons 1 and 2 you will write sentences with spaces after particles and between words in order to make them easier to read. From Lesson 3 on, however, you will write in the continuous style, without spaces, which is the customary way of writing Japanese.

    In the reading exercises, you are introduced to dialogues in a natural conversational style, so that you can gain some proficiency in the spoken language while learning to read and write, thus killing two birds with one stone. The exercises here are arranged so that you can gradually become accustomed to writing in the vertical style.

    Note that the symbol ⏺ indicates sections that are recorded on the accompanying cassette tape.

KATAKANA

- Coming to grips with the forms of *katakana*

    Katakana are so simple in form that you may find it difficult to memorize them. For this reason, we start by providing some visual clues. First of all, we introduce *katakana* that resemble their *hiragana* equivalents. Then we categorize the other *katakana* into groups of similar shapes.
- Reading and writing

    The exercises here are much the same as those for *hiragana*, which you will have already completed and become familiar with.
- Words written in *katakana*

    The words forming the exercises in this section will be restricted to the names of common, everyday objects.
- Transliteration of foreign words

    One function of *katakana* is to transliterate foreign words into Japanese. Here you will be given a few guidelines to help you with this not-always-easy task.

HIRAGANA
1

BASIC SYLLABLES
Pronunciation
The Vowels

a	i	u	e	o
あ	い	う	え	お
ア	イ	ウ	エ	オ

The first line of the syllabary consists of the five vowels *a, i, u, e, o.* They are short vowels, enunciated clearly and crisply. Pronounce the English sentence below, making all of the vowels short, and you will have the approximate sounds. The *u* is pronounced without moving the lips forward. The *o* is similar to the initial sound of "old," but it isn't a diphthong, so don't round the lips.

Ah, we soon get old.
a   i   u   e   o

Consonants plus vowel and *n*

The rest of syllabary consists of syllables formed by a consonant and a vowel. Most Japanese consonants are pronounced with the lips or the tip of the tongue more relaxed than in English. For example, if the *t* in *kite* is pronounced too strongly and with a good deal of aspiration, it will be heard as *kitte.* So be especially careful to pronounce *p, t,* and *k* with less aspiration than in English.

	a	i	u	e	o
k	か	き	く	け	こ
	カ	キ	ク	ケ	コ
g	が	ぎ	ぐ	げ	ご
	ガ	ギ	グ	ゲ	ゴ
s	さ	し shi	す	せ	そ
	サ	シ	ス	セ	ソ
z	ざ	じ ji	ず zu	ぜ	ぞ
	ザ	ジ	ズ	ゼ	ゾ

The consonant *k* is pronounced more softly than in English.

At the beginning of a word, the *g* in *ga, gi, gu, ge, go* is hard (like the "g" in "garden"), but when occurring in the middle of a word or in the last syllable, it is often nasal, as in *eiga* ("movie"). The particle *ga,* too, is usually nasalized, though nowadays many people use a hard *g.*

The breath is expelled less forcefully in the Japanese consonant than the English. *Shi* is a near equivalent of the English "she," but is enunciated with the lips unrounded. Note that there is no Japanese syllable *si.*

The breath is expelled less forcefully with the Japanese consonant than the English. When *za, zu, ze, zo* come at the beginning of a word, the *z* is affricative, sounding like "ds" in "kids." In the middle of a word or in the last syllable, however, it is fricative, sounding like the "z" in "zoo." *Ji* is an affricate at the beginning of a word, like the "je" in "jeep," but fricative in a middle position, like "si" in "vision." Note that Japanese doesn't have the syllable *zi.*

	a	i	u	e	o
t	た タ	ち **chi** チ	つ **tsu** ツ	て テ	と ト
d	だ ダ	ぢ **ji** ヂ	づ **zu** ヅ	で デ	ど ド
n	な ナ	に ニ	ぬ ヌ	ね ネ	の ノ
h	は ハ	ひ ヒ	ふ **fu** フ	へ へ	ほ ホ
b	ば バ	び ビ	ぶ ブ	べ ベ	ぼ ボ
p	ぱ パ	ぴ ピ	ぷ プ	ぺ ペ	ぽ ポ
m	ま マ	み ミ	む ム	め メ	も モ

The aspiration of this consonant is weaker than in English. *Chi* is pronounced like "chi" in "children." *Tsu* is pronounced with the consonant *ts* similar to the "ts" in "cats." Note that Japanese doesn't have the syllables *ti* or *tu*.

ぢ and づ are pronounced *ji* and *zu*. The syllable *di* and *du* do not exist. In general, *ji* and *zu* are written じ and ず, but in a few rare cases custom calls for ぢ and づ.

This consonant is similar to the "n" in "nice," but is less prolonged.

The breath is not expelled as strongly as in English. In *fu,* the consonant is made differently from the "f" in English "foot." It is produced by expelling air through lightly compressed lips, much like blowing out a candle.

This consonant is pronounced nearly the same as English "b."

This consonant is pronounced with less aspiration than English "p."

This consonant is similar to the "m" in "mind," though not quite as prolonged.

	a	**i**	**u**	**e**	**o**
y	や ヤ		ゆ ユ		よ ヨ

Japanese *y* is pronounced with the tongue in a more relaxed position than the "y" in "year."

r	ら ラ	り リ	る ル	れ レ	ろ ロ

Japanese *r* is produced by tapping the tip of the tongue lightly against the teethridge. It is never pronounced with the tip of the tongue curled back.

w	わ ワ				を ヲ

W is pronounced with the lips rounded, but not so tightly or forcefully as with the "w" in "wait."

n	ん ン				

N is the only independent consonant not combined with a vowel. Occurring at the end of a word, it has a somewhat nasal sound. Otherwise it approximates the English "n." If it is followed by syllables beginning with *b, m,* or *p,* however, it is pronounced more like "m," and is accordingly spelled as an "m" in this book. Special care is needed when the syllabic *n* is followed by a vowel, as in the word *kin'en* (*ki-n-en,* "no smoking"). Note the difference in syllable division between this word and *kinen* (*ki-ne-n,* "anniversary").

Recognition of Forms

あいうえお　かきくけこ　さしすせそ

Find the parenthetical syllables in the rows at right.

（あ）ゆ お よ あ ぬ お　（い）い に こ い り い
a　　　　　　　　　　　　i

（う）え う ろ ら う ら　（え）ん え よん く え
u　　　　　　　　　　　　e

（お）あ よ は お ま お　（か）が か け が あ か
o　　　　　　　　　　　　ka

（き）ま さ き ざ き ぎ　（く）し へ く ぐ し く
ki　　　　　　　　　　　　ku

（け）は け ほ げ は け　（こ）こ い に い ご こ
ke　　　　　　　　　　　　ko

（さ）き さ ざ せ さ き　（し）く し へん じ し
sa　　　　　　　　　　　　shi

（す）ま す む よ す ず　（せ）せ さ や ぜ さ や
su　　　　　　　　　　　　se

（そ）え そ ろ ぞ ら そ
so

（あ）（い）（う）あ り こ い あ ろ う ら こ お い う お あい
a　　i　　u

（き）（く）（え）さ し え き ぐん ぎ く へ く き さ え べ き
ki　ku　e

（す）（そ）（お）ま ろ そ よ す あ ず そ お ろ す お あ そ す
su　so　o

（せ）（け）（か）や せ は け ほ が か お に け ぜ か け や せ
se　ke　ka

Reading (answers given below)

1. あか　2. いえ　3. かぐ　4. しお　5. かぎ　6. あお

1. **aka** (red)　2. **ie** (house)　3. **kagu** (furniture)　4. **shio** (salt)　5. **kagi** (key)　6. **ao** (blue)

たちつてと　　なにぬねの　　はひふへほ

Find the parenthetical syllables in the rows at right.

(た) に こ ⓣ な に こ　　(ち) ろ う る ⓒ ら ⓒ
ta　　　　　　　　　　　chi

(つ) し う ⓣ く て ⓣ　　(て) し で こ ⓣ く ⓣ
tsu　　　　　　　　　　te

(と) を ⓣ て ⓣ ち と　　(な) た ⓝ ば ⓝ は ⓝ
to　　　　　　　　　　　na

(に) ⓝ た こ ⓝ い こ　　(ぬ) ね め ⓝ ⓝ な わ
ni　　　　　　　　　　　nu

(ね) め わ ⓝ れ ⓝ わ　　(の) め ⓝ ね ⓝ め ⓝ
ne　　　　　　　　　　　no

(は) ば ⓗ ぱ け ま ⓗ　　(ひ) ぴ ⓗ び ⓗ ぴ ⓗ
ha　　　　　　　　　　　hi

(ふ) そ ⓕ ぷ へ ぶ ⓕ　　(へ) つ ⓗ ぺ く ⓗ べ
fu　　　　　　　　　　　he

(ほ) は ま ⓗ ば ⓗ ぼ
ho

(た) (な) (は) に な ほ ば た は け ぼ な た は な た な は
ta　na　ha

(で) (ど) (べ) と で へ を ど し べ ご ぺ て へ で と ど ぺ
de　do　be

(て) (に) (の) た の て で に の こ く て に め の に で た
te　ni　no

(つ) (ぬ) (ち) し め つ ち ら ね へ つ ぬ め し く さ ち ぬ
tsu　nu　chi

🎞

Reading

1. はな　　2. おかね　　3. さかな

---

1. **hana** (flower)　2. **okane** (money)　3. **sakana** (fish)

14

Find the parenthetical syllables in the rows at right.

(ま) よ ま き ま ほ ま
ma

(み) ゆ の み み お み
mi

(む) ぬ す め む す む
mu

(め) の ぬ め あ ぬ め
me

(も) も ま し と も ほ
mo

(や) せ や せ さ や せ
ya

(ゆ) の ゆ る ゆ ひ の
yu

(よ) ま ゆ よ ろ す よ
yo

(ら) ろ そ う る ら ち
ra

(り) い り こ り い り
ri

(る) ら る ろ り ら る
ru

(れ) れ わ ね れ わ め
re

(ろ) そ ろ ら ち ろ ら
ro

(わ) れ わ ね め あ わ
wa

(を) と を と を て を
o

(ん) ん え て ん え ん
n

(ま)(よ)(も) お ま ほ も ば よ す よ き ま も お も ま も
ma yo mo

(ら)(ろ)(る) る そ う ら ろ ち る え ら み ろ ら お ろ る
ra ro ru

(め)(わ)(れ) れ ぬ め ね わ む め ま ろ わ を れ め ね あ
me wa re

(を)(と)(て) さ と つ て を き へ て で と ど を て ど へ
o to te

(く)(し)(つ) く ぐ じ つ へ し け じ く つ へ て づ し ぐ
ku shi tsu

(は)(ほ)(ま) ぼ ま は は よ す ほ ば ま け に は ま よ ほ
ha ho ma

Reading

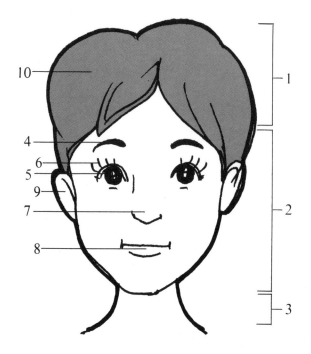

1. あたま

2. かお

3. くび

4. まゆげ

5. め

6. まつげ

7. はな

8. くち

9. みみ

10. かみの け

11. わたしの め

12. わたしの かお

Common Japanese Names

13. たなか　　14. すずき　　15. きくち　　16. みやざき

17. まつもと　　18. わたなべ　　19. ふくだ　　20. ぬまた

21. うえださんと やまださん

Listen to the tape and become thoroughly familiar with the pronunciation. Note that the vowel sounds *i* and *u* are unvoiced when they come between unvoiced consonants (*p, t, k, s*) or between an unvoiced consonant and a pause.

---

1. **atama** (head)　2. **kao** (face)　3. **kubi** (neck)　4. **mayuge** (eyebrow)　5. **me** (eye)
6. **matsuge** (eyelashes)　7. **hana** (nose)　8. **kuchi** (mouth)　9. **mimi** (ear)
10. **kami no ke** (hair)　11. **watashi no me** (my eye[s])　12. **watashi no kao** (my face)
13. **Tanaka**　14. **Suzuki**　15. **Kikuchi**　16. **Miyazaki**　17. **Matsumoto**
18. **Watanabe**　19. **Fukuda**　20. **Numata**　21. **Ueda-san to Yamada-san**
(Mr./Mrs./Miss/Ms. Ueda and Mr./Mrs./Miss/Ms. Yamada)

Writing

The gray lines are aids to accurate style. In writing *kana*, the stroke order is, as a rule, first from top to bottom, then from left to right.

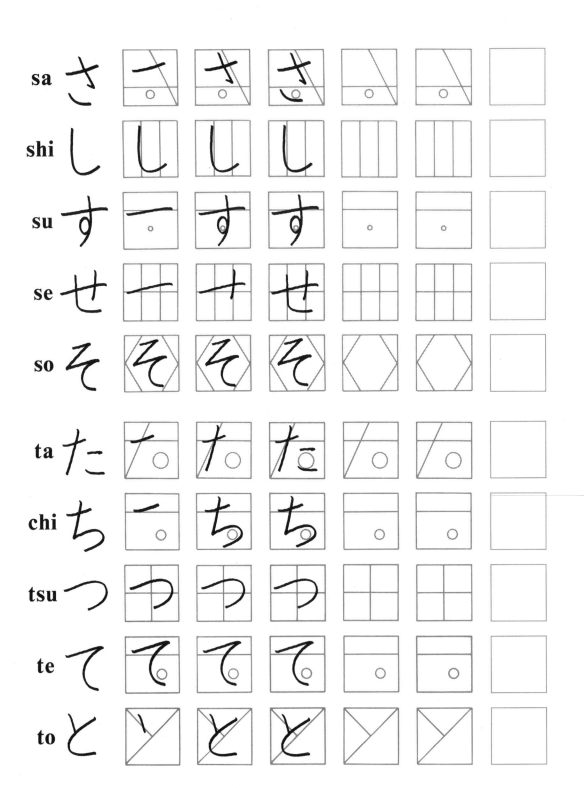

sa	さ
shi	し
su	す
se	せ
so	そ
ta	た
chi	ち
tsu	つ
te	て
to	と

18

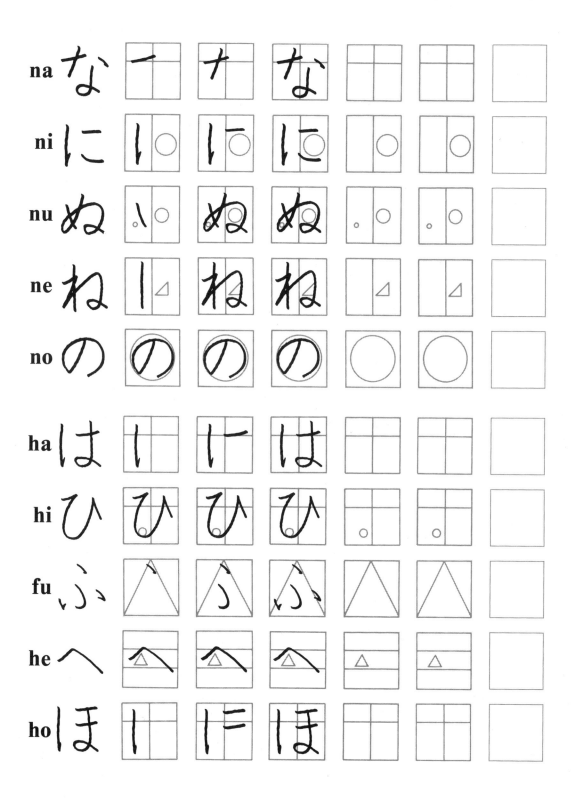

na	な
ni	に
nu	ぬ
ne	ね
no	の
ha	は
hi	ひ
fu	ふ
he	へ
ho	ほ

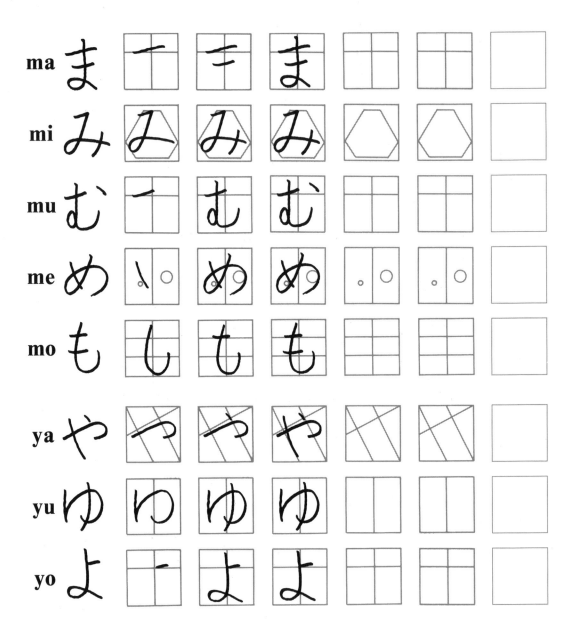

ma	ま
mi	み
mu	む
me	め
mo	も
ya	や
yu	ゆ
yo	よ

20

ra	ら
ri	り
ru	る
re	れ
ro	ろ
wa	わ
o	を
n	ん

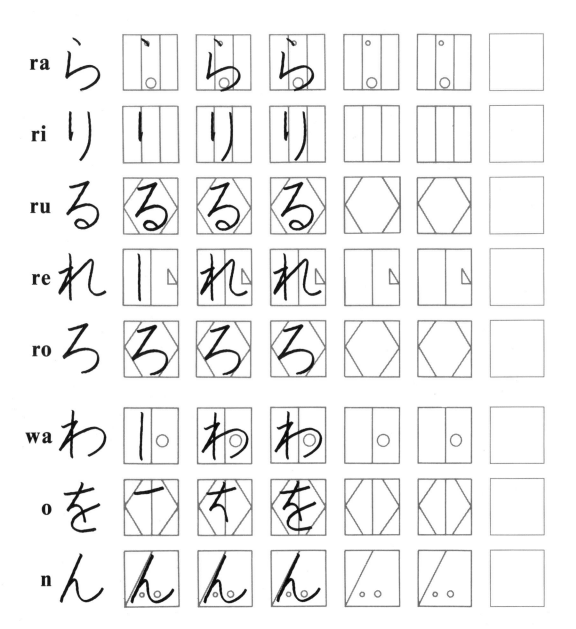

The ゛ and ゜ markings of が, ぱ, etc. should be written at the upper right-hand corner of these syllables. Write the following *hiragana*, following the examples.

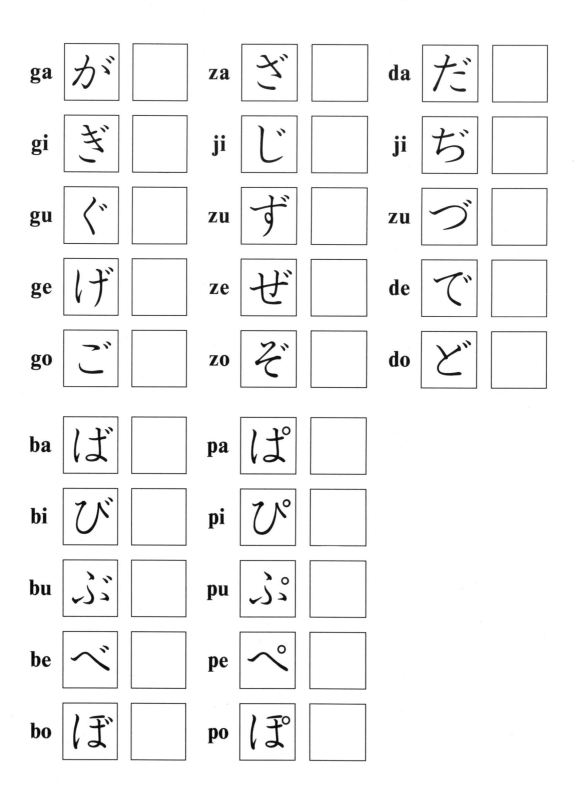

ga	が		za	ざ		da	だ	
gi	ぎ		ji	じ		ji	ぢ	
gu	ぐ		zu	ず		zu	づ	
ge	げ		ze	ぜ		de	で	
go	ご		zo	ぞ		do	ど	

ba	ば		pa	ぱ	
bi	び		pi	ぴ	
bu	ぶ		pu	ぷ	
be	べ		pe	ぺ	
bo	ぼ		po	ぽ	

Reading and Writing

The following pairs consist of look-alike syllables. Read, write, and distinguish them.

あ お　**a o**

き さ　**ki sa**

ぬ ね　**nu ne**

て こ　**te ko**

し も　**shi mo**

る ろ　**ru ro**

ほ は　**ho ha**

た な　**ta na**

つ と　**tsu to**

う つ　**u tsu**

こ い　**ko i**

ま ほ　**ma ho**

め ぬ　**me nu**

へ て　**he te**

り い　**ri i**

す む　**su mu**

え ふ　**e fu**

そ て　**so te**

Reading and Writing

First read the words, covering the romanization. Then write them, covering the *hiragana*.

1. うち   **uchi**

2. くるま   **kuruma**

3. かさ   **kasa**

4. しごと   **shigoto**

5. みず   **mizu**

6. かぎ   **kagi**

7. べんごし   **bengoshi**

8. なつ   **natsu**

9. ひと   **hito**

10. ほん   **hon**

11. でんち   **denchi**

12. みかん   **mikan**

---

1. house, home   2. car, vehicle   3. umbrella   4. job, work   5. water   6. key   7. lawyer
8. summer   9. person   10. book   11. battery   12. tangerine

MODIFIED SYLLABLES

Pronunciation: Consonants plus *ya, yu, yo*

Although the following are written with two *kana*, they are pronounced as single syllables. The *y*, which sounds like the "y" in "year," is pronounced between the initial consonant and the following vowel.

	ya	yu	yo
k	きゃ キャ	きゅ キュ	きょ キョ
g	ぎゃ ギャ	ぎゅ ギュ	ぎょ ギョ
s	しゃ **sha** シャ	しゅ **shu** シュ	しょ **sho** ショ
j	じゃ **ja** ジャ	じゅ **ju** ジュ	じょ **jo** ジョ
c	ちゃ **cha** チャ	ちゅ **chu** チュ	ちょ **cho** チョ
n	にゃ ニャ	にゅ ニュ	にょ ニョ

	ya	yu	yo
h	ひゃ ヒャ	ひゅ ヒュ	ひょ ヒョ
b	びゃ ビャ	びゅ ビュ	びょ ビョ
p	ぴゃ ピャ	ぴゅ ピュ	ぴょ ピョ
m	みゃ ミャ	みゅ ミュ	みょ ミョ
r	りゃ リャ	りゅ リュ	りょ リョ

Writing

Although, as you have already learned, a consonant plus *ya, yu*, or *yo* is pronounced as a single syllable, it is written with two *kana* and occupies the space for two characters. In such cases, *ya, yu*, and *yo* are written small, approximately one-fourth the size of a normal *kana*. In horizontal writing, they are written small in the lower left quadrant of the square. In vertical writing, they appear small in the upper right quadrant. Write the following *hiragana*, following the examples.

kya	きゃ					
kyu	きゅ					
kyo	きょ					
gya	ぎゃ					
gyu	ぎゅ					
gyo	ぎょ					
sha	しゃ					
shu	しゅ					
sho	しょ					
ja	じゃ					
ju	じゅ					
jo	じょ					

cha	ちゃ				
chu	ちゅ				
cho	ちょ				
nya	にゃ				
nyu	にゅ				
nyo	にょ				
hya	ひゃ				
hyu	ひゅ				
hyo	ひょ				
bya	びゃ				
byu	びゅ				
byo	びょ				
pya	ぴゃ				
pyu	ぴゅ				
pyo	ぴょ				

ちゃ		
ちゅ		
ちょ		
にゃ		
にゅ		
にょ		
ひゃ		
ひゅ		

mya	み や					
myu	み ゅ					
myo	み ょ					
rya	り ゃ					
ryu	り ゅ					
ryo	り ょ					

ひ ょ		
み ゃ		
み ゅ		
み ょ		
り ゃ		
り ゅ		
り ょ		

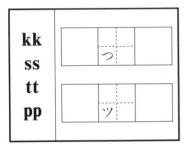

OTHER SYLLABLES

Pronunciation

Long Vowels

ā	ああ アー
ī	いい イー
ū	うう ウー
ē	ええ　えい エー
ō	おお　おう オー

Long vowels are a doubling of single vowels. Be particularly careful to pronounce them as a continuous sound, equal in value to two short vowels. The way long vowels are written varies from case to case. With *aa, ii, uu*, the single vowel is simply doubled: ああ, いい, うう. *Ee* is most often written えい, though ええ is also seen. *Oo* is generally おう, but some words customarily demand おお. The same rules apply when a consonant is followed by a long vowel: e.g., *kaa* (かあ), *kii* (きい), *kuu* (くう), *kee* (けい, けえ), *koo* (こう, こお).

Double Consonants

kk ss tt pp	っ ッ

The first consonant of the double consonants *kk, pp, tt,* and *ss* is written with a small っ. っ here indicates a one-syllable pause, during which the mouth prepares itself for the pronunciation of the next syllable. Take *kitte*, for example. After pronouncing *ki*, pause for the length of one syllable, shaping your mouth for the pronunciation of *te*. And then pronounce it—*te*. With *ss*, as in *zasshi*, see that a small amount of air is emitted between the teeth before pronouncing the following syllable. The small っ and ッ that indicate double consonants are written in different quadrants according to whether the text is horizontal or vertical.

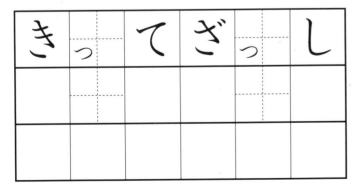

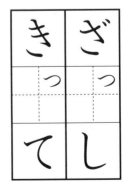

Reading and Writing

FATHER'S DIARY

3がつ (March)		sangatsu
10 (Mon.)	げつようび	getsu-yōbi
11 (Tues.)	かようび　　　①かいぎ	ka-yōbi
12 (Wed.)	すいようび	sui-yōbi
13 (Thurs.)	もくようび	moku-yōbi
14 (Fri.)	きんようび	kin-yōbi
15 (Sat.)	どようび　　　②えいが	do-yōbi
16 (Sun.)	にちようび	nichi-yōbi

MY FAMILY

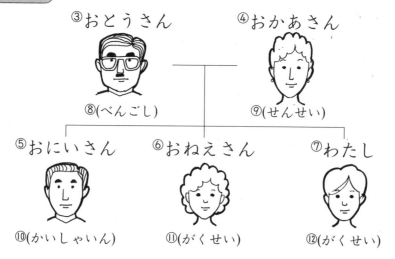

③おとうさん　　　　④おかあさん
⑧(べんごし)　　　　⑨(せんせい)

⑤おにいさん　　⑥おねえさん　　⑦わたし
⑩(かいしゃいん)　⑪(がくせい)　⑫(がくせい)

---

① **kaigi** (meeting)　② **eiga** (movie)　③ **otō-san** (father)　④ **okā-san** (mother)
⑤ **onī-san** (elder brother)　⑥ **onē-san** (elder sister)　⑦ **watashi** (I, me)　⑧ **bengoshi** (lawyer)
⑨ **sensei** (teacher)　⑩ **kaishain** (company employee)　⑪⑫ **gakusei** (student)

Reading

A) 1. ひとつ 2. ふたつ 3. みっつ

4. よっつ 5. いつつ 6. むっつ

7. ななつ 8. やっつ 9. ここのつ

10. とお

---

11. いっぽん 12. いっぷん 13. ごふん

14. ざっし 15. きって 16. きっぷ

B) 1. きょう 2. しゅうまつ 3. かいしゃ

4. ひしょ 5. おちゃ 6. じゅうしょ

7. ゆうびんきょく 8. しゃしん 9. とうきょう

10. ちゅうごく 11. しゃちょう 12. りょこう

13. びょういん 14. ごしゅじん 15. たんじょうび

A) 1. **hitotsu** (one) 2. **futatsu** (two) 3. **mittsu** (three) 4. **yottsu** (four) 5. **itsutsu** (five) 6. **muttsu** (six) 7. **nanatsu** (seven) 8. **yattsu** (eight) 9. **kokonotsu** (nine) 10. **tō** (ten) 11. **ippon** (one bottle, pencil, etc.) 12. **ippun** (one minute) 13. **gofun** (five minutes) 14. **zasshi** (magazine) 15. **kitte** (stamp) 16. **kippu** (ticket)

B) 1. **kyō** (today) 2. **shūmatsu** (weekend) 3. **kaisha** (company) 4. **hisho** (secretary) 5. **ocha** (tea) 6. **jūsho** (address) 7. **yūbinkyoku** (post office) 8. **shashin** (picture) 9. **Tōkyō** (Tokyo) 10. **Chūgoku** (China) 11. **shachō** (president) 12. **ryokō** (travel) 13. **byōin** (hospital) 14. **goshujin** (your/his/her husband) 15. **tanjōbi** (birthday)

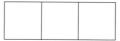

Reading and Writing

First, read the words, covering the romanization. Then write the words, covering the *hiragana*.

1. いっぷん **ippun**

2. じゅうしょ **jūsho**

3. やっつ **yattsu**

4. きって **kitte**

5. りょこう **ryokō**

6. すいようび **sui-yōbi**

7. おにいさん **onīsan**

8. ひしょ **hisho**

---

1. one minute　　2. address　　3. eight　　4. stamp
5. trip　　6. Wednesday　　7. (older) brother　　8. secretary

9. めいし   **meishi**   ☐☐☐

10. せんせい   **sensei**   ☐☐☐☐

11. きのう   **kinō**   ☐☐☐

12. でんしゃ   **densha**   ☐☐☐☐

13. ばんごう   **bangō**   ☐☐☐☐

14. たんじょうび   **tanjōbi**   ☐☐☐☐☐☐

15. とけい   **tokei**   ☐☐☐

16. 5じ10ぷん   **goji juppun** | 5 | | 10 | | |

---

9. calling (business) card   10. teacher   11. yesterday
12. train   13. number   14. birthday
15. watch, clock   16. ten minutes after five

1. おげんきですか。

　　　　はい、げんきです。

2. どうもありがとうございます。

　　　　どういたしまして。

3. いってきます。

　　　　いってらっしゃい。

4. ただいま。

　　　　おかえりなさい。

5. さようなら。

　　　　しつれいします。

---

1. **O-genki desu ka.** (How are you?) **Hai, genki desu.** (Fine, thank you.)
2. **Dōmo arigatō gozaimasu.** (Thank you very much.) **Dō itashimashite.** (You are welcome.)
3. **Itte kimasu.** (I'm going.) **Itte rasshai.** (See you later.)
4. **Tadaima.** (I'm back [home].) **Okaerinasai.** (Welcome back [home].)
5. **Sayōnara.** (Good-bye.) **Shitsurei shimasu.** (Good-bye.)

Writing

Write the sentences, following the examples. The punctuation 、 and 。 occupy one square. When writing horizontally, they are written in the lower left-hand quadrant. See p. 52 for vertical writing.

1. | お | げ | ん | き | で | す | か | 。 |

| | | | | | | | |

| は | い | 、 | げ | ん | き | で | す | 。 |

| | | | | | | | | |

2. | ど | う | も | あ | り | が | と | う | ご | ざ | い | ま | す | 。 |

| | | | | | | | | | | | | | |

| ど | う | い | た | し | ま | し | て | 。 |

| | | | | | | | | |

---

1. **O-genki desu ka.** (How are you?)
   Hai, genki desu. (I'm fine.)
2. **Dōmo arigatō gozaimasu.** (Thank you.)
   Dō itashimashite. (You're welcome.)

HIRAGANA

2

LESSON 1

Reading

| STRUCTURE | ～は～です。 |

1. これは　ほんです。

2. それは　はなです。

3. あれは　かさです。

4. あれは　ぎんこうです。

5. わたしは　たなかです。

6. たなかさんは　にほんじんです。

Note that the particle *wa* is written は, not わ. When reading aloud, pause slightly after the particles.

Writing (Write the sentences, following the examples.)

1.
こ	れ	は	は	な	で	す	。

2.
あ	れ	は	ぎ	ん	こ	う	で	す	。

3.
た	な	か	さ	ん	は	に	ほ	ん	じ	ん	で	す	。

---

1. **Kore wa hon desu.** (This is a book.)
2. **Sore wa hana desu.** (That is a flower.)
3. **Are wa kasa desu.** (That is an umbrella.)
4. **Are wa ginkō desu.** (That is a bank.)
5. **Watashi wa Tanaka desu.** (My name is Tanaka. [I'm Tanaka.])
6. **Tanaka-san wa Nihon-jin desu.** (Mr. Tanaka is a Japanese.)

Reading

I A：これは　なんですか。

    B：それは　かぎです。

    A：これも　かぎですか。

    B：いいえ、それは　めいしです。

II A：かとうさんですか。

    B：はい、かとうです。

    A：たなかです。はじめまして。どうぞよろしく。

    B：かとうです。どうぞよろしく。

I A. **Kore wa nan desu ka.** (What's this?)
    B. **Sore wa kagi desu.** (That's a key.)
    A. **Kore mo kagi desu ka.** (Is this also a key?)
    B. **Iie, sore wa meishi desu.** (No, that's a business card.)
      Note that めいし (**meishi**) is pronouced **mēshi**, with a long **ē**.
II A. **Katō-san desu ka.** (Are you Mr. Kato?)
    B. **Hai, Katō desu.** (Yes, I am.)
    A. **Tanaka desu. Hajimemashite. Dōzo yoroshiku.** (My name's Tanaka. How do you do?
      I'm very glad to meet you.)
    B. **Katō desu. Dōzo yoroshiku.** (My name's Kato. Nice to meet you.)

LESSON 2

Reading

1. これは　わたしの　くるまです。

2. それは　たなかさんの　とけいです。

3. あれは　はやしさんのです。

4. やまださんは　かとうさんの　ひしょです。

5. こちらは　とうきょうでんきの　たなかさんです。

6. これは　うちの　でんわばんごうです。

Writing

1. | こ | れ | は | わ | た | し | の | く | る | ま | で | す | 。 |
   |---|---|---|---|---|---|---|---|---|---|---|---|---|
   | | | | | | | | | | | | | |

2. | や | ま | だ | さ | ん | は | か | と | う | さ | ん | の | ひ | し | ょ |
   |---|---|---|---|---|---|---|---|---|---|---|---|---|---|---|
   | で | す | 。 | | | | | | | | | | | | |

---

1. **Kore wa watashi no kuruma desu.** (This is my car.)
2. **Sore wa Tanaka-san no tokei desu.** (That's Mr. Tanaka's watch.)
3. **Are wa Hayashi-san no desu.** (That's Mr. Hayashi's.)
4. **Yamada-san wa Katō-san no hisho desu.** (Ms. Yamada is Mr. Kato's secretary.)
5. **Kochira wa Tōkyō Denki no Tanaka-san desu.** (This is Mr. Tanaka from Tokyo Electric.)
6. **Kore wa uchi no denwa-bangō desu.** (This is my home telephone number.)

Reading

I　A：これは　ゆかわさんの　くるまですか。

　　B：ええ、わたしのです。

　　A：あれは　どなたのですか。

　　B：あれは　かわむらさんの　くるまです。

II　A：わたしの　めいしです。どうぞ。

　　B：どうも　ありがとうございます。
　　　　これは　かいしゃの　でんわばんごうですか。

　　A：いいえ、それは　うちのです。
　　　　かいしゃの　でんわばんごうは　451-7699です。

III　A：ごしょうかいします。こちらは　ぬまたさんです。
　　　　ぬまたさんは　とうきょうでんきの　べんごしです。

　　B：ぬまたです。はじめまして。どうぞよろしく。

　　A：こちらは　ねぎしさんです。
　　　　ねぎしさんは　はやしさんの　ひしょです。

　　C：はじめまして。ねぎしです。どうぞよろしく。

I　A. **Kore wa Yukawa-san no kuruma desu ka.** (Is this your car, Mr. Yukawa?)
　B. **Ee, watashi no desu.** (Yes, it's mine.)
　A. **Are wa donata no desu ka.** (Whose is that?)
　B. **Are wa Kawamura-san no kuruma desu.** (That's Mr. Kawamura's car.)

II　A. **Watashi no meishi desu.** (This is my business card.) **Dōzo.** (Please [take it].)
　B. **Dōmo arigatō gozaimasu.** (Thank you very much.)
　　Kore wa kaisha no denwa-bangō desu ka. (Is this your company's telephone number?)
　A. **Iie, sore wa uchi no desu. Kaisha no denwa-bangō wa**
　　yon-gō-ichi-no-nana-roku-kyū-kyū desu.
　　(No, that's my home number. The company's number is 451-7699.)

III　A. **Go-shōkai shimasu. Kochira wa Numata-san desu.** (Let me introduce you. This is Mr. Numata.)
　　Numata-san wa Tōkyō Denki no bengoshi desu. (Mr. Numata is a lawyer at Tokyo Electric.)
　B. **Numata desu. Hajimemashite. Dōzo yoroshiku.** (I'm Numata. How do you do?)
　A. **Kochira wa Negishi-san desu. Negishi-san wa Hayashi-san no hisho desu.** (This is Ms. Negishi. She is Mr. Hayashi's secretary.)
　C. **Hajimemashite. Negishi desu. Dōzo yoroshiku.** (How do you do? I'm Negishi. I'm very glad to meet you.)

LESSON 3

Reading

| STRUCTURE | 〜は〜では　ありません。 |

1. これは わたしの ほんでは ありません。

2. それは うちの じゅうしょでは ありません。

3. きむらさんは かいしゃいんでは ありません。

4. あれは にほんの くるまでは ありません。

5. これは きょうの しんぶんでは ありません。

6. この きっては ちゅうごくのでは ありません。

Note that *dewa* is written では, not でわ.

Writing

1.
そ	れ	は	う	ち	の	じ	ゅ	う	し	ょ	で	は
あ	り	ま	せ	ん	。							

2.
こ	の	き	っ	て	は	ち	ゅ	う	ご	く	の	で	は
あ	り	ま	せ	ん	。								

---

1. **Kore wa watashi no hon dewa arimasen.** (This is not my book.)
2. **Sore wa uchi no jūsho dewa arimasen.** (That is not my home address.)
3. **Kimura-san wa kaishain dewa arimasen.** (Mr. Kimura is not a company employee.)
4. **Are wa Nihon no kuruma dewa arimasen.** (That is not a Japanese car.)
5. **Kore wa kyō no shimbun dewa arimasen.** (This is not today's newspaper.)
6. **Kono kitte wa Chūgoku no dewa arimasen.** (This postage stamp is not a Chinese one.)

Reading

I A：この　えいがは　にほんの　えいがですか。

　 B：いいえ、にほんのでは　ありません。

　 A：どこの　えいがですか。

　 B：ちゅうごくのです。

II A：これは　ゆうびんきょくの　でんわばんごうですか。

　 B：いいえ、ゆうびんきょくのでは　ありません。

　 A：ゆうびんきょくの　でんわばんごうは　なんばんですか。

　 B：788-9904です。

　 A：がっこうの　でんわばんごうは？

　 B：がっこうの　でんわばんごうは　226-8768です。

I A. **Kono eiga wa Nihon no eiga desu ka.** (Is this a Japanese movie?)
　B. **Iie, Nihon no dewa arimasen.** (No, it's not.)
　A. **Doko no eiga desu ka.** (Where is the movie from?/Where was the movie made?)
　B. **Chūgoku no desu.** (It's a Chinese movie.)
II A. **Kore wa yūbinkyoku no denwa-bangō desu ka.** (Is this the telephone number of the post office?)
　B. **Iie, yūbinkyoku no dewa arimasen.** (No, it's not the post office's.)
　A. **Yūbinkyoku no denwa-bangō wa nan-ban desu ka.** (What is the telephone number of the post office?)
　B. **Nana-hachi-hachi-no-kyū-kyū-zero-yon desu.** (It's 788-9904.)
　A. **Gakkō no denwa-bangō wa ?** (What about the telephone number of the school?)
　B. **Gakkō no denwa-bangō wa ni-ni-roku-no-hachi-nana-roku-hachi desu.** (The telephone number of the school is 226-8768.)

LESSON 4

Reading

STRUCTURE	～から～まで

1. かいしゃは　9じ<u>から</u>　5じ<u>まで</u>です。

2. ぎんこうは　ごぜん　9じ<u>から</u>　ごご　3じ<u>まで</u>です。

3. かいぎは　ごぜん　8じはん<u>から</u>　11じ<u>まで</u>です。

4. ひるやすみは　12じ<u>から</u>　ごご　1じ15ふん<u>まで</u>です。

5. なつやすみは　7がつ　15にち<u>から</u>　8がつ　30にち<u>まで</u>です。

6. やすみは　もくようび<u>から</u>　げつようび<u>まで</u>です。

Writing (Write the following romanized sentences in *hiragana*.)

Kaisha wa ku-ji kara go-ji made desu.

Kaigi wa gozen hachi-ji han kara jūichi-ji made desu.

Natsu-yasumi wa shichi-gatsu jūgo-nichi kara desu.

---

1. **Kaisha wa ku-ji kara go-ji made desu.** (Office hours are from 9:00 to 5:00.)
2. **Ginkō wa gozen ku-ji kara gogo san-ji made desu.** (Banks are open from 9 A.M. to 3 P.M.)
3. **Kaigi wa gozen hachi-ji han kara jūichi-ji made desu.** (The meeting is from 8:30 in the morning to 11:00.)
4. **Hiru-yasumi wa jūni-ji kara gogo ichi-ji jūgo-fun made desu.** (Lunch time is from 12:00 to 1:15 P.M.)
5. **Natsu-yasumi wa shichi-gatsu jūgo-nichi kara hachi-gatsu sanjū-nichi made desu.** (Summer vacation is from July 15 till August 30.)
6. **Yasumi wa moku-yōbi kara getsu-yōbi made desu.** (Our vacation is from Thursday to Monday./We are on vacation from Thursday to Monday.)

Reading

I A：いま　なんじですか。

　　B：7じはんです。

　　A：がっこうは　なんじからですか。

　　B：8じからです。

II A：ひるやすみは　なんじまでですか。

　　B：1じ20ぷんまでです。

　　A：かいぎは　なんじから　なんじまでですか。

　　B：ごご　2じはんから　4じまでです。

III A：すぎうらさんは　きょう　やすみですか。

　　B：ええ。きのうから　すぎうらさんは　なつやすみです。

　　A：すぎうらさんの　なつやすみは　いつまでですか。

　　B：8がつ　25にちまでです。

I A. **Ima nan-ji desu ka.** (What time is it now?)
B. **Shichi-ji han desu.** (It's 7:30.)
A. **Gakkō wa nan-ji kara desu ka.** (What time does school start?)
B. **Hachi-ji kara desu.** (It begins at 8:00.)
II A. **Hiru-yasumi wa nan-ji made desu ka.** (What time [when] does lunch time end?)
B. **Ichi-ji nijuppun made desu.** (It ends at 1:20.)
A. **Kaigi wa nan-ji kara nan-ji made desu ka.** (What time does the meeting begin and end?)
B. **Gogo ni-ji han kara yo-ji made desu.** (It's from 2:30 to 4:00 P.M.)
III A. **Sugiura-san wa kyō yasumi desu ka.** (Is Mr. Sugiura off today?)
B. **Ee. Kinō kara Sugiura-san wa natsu-yasumi desu.** (Yes, he went on summer vacation yesterday.)
A. **Sugiura-san no natsu-yasumi wa itsu made desu ka.** (How long will Mr. Sugiura's summer vacation last?)
B. **Hachi-gatsu nijūgo-nichi made desu.** (Until August 25th.)

LESSON 5

Reading

STRUCTURE	～を　ください。

1. みず<u>を</u>　<u>ください</u>。

2. くろい　かさ<u>を</u>　<u>ください</u>。

3. その　あかい　はな<u>を</u>　10ぽん　<u>ください</u>。

4. この　りんご<u>を</u>　むっつ　<u>ください</u>。

5. 62えんの　きって<u>を</u>　10まい　<u>ください</u>。

6. あの　おおきい　とけい<u>を</u>　みせて　<u>ください</u>。

Note that the particle *o* is written を, not お.

Writing

Mizu o kudasai.

Kono ringo o muttsu kudasai.

Rokujūni-en no kitte o jū-mai kudasai.

Ano ōkii tokei o misete kudasai.

---

1. **Mizu o kudasai.** (Please give me some water./Water, please.)
2. **Kuroi kasa o kudasai.** (Please give me a black umbrella./I'd like a black umbrella.)
3. **Sono akai hana o juppon kudasai.** (Please give me ten of those red flowers.)
4. **Kono ringo o muttsu kudasai.** (Please give me six of these apples.)
5. **Rokujūni-en no kitte o jū-mai kudasai.** (Please give me ten ¥62 postage stamps.)
6. **Ano ōkii tokei o misete kudasai.** (Please show me that big clock.)

Reading

I A：この　でんちは　いくらですか。

　　B：それは　ひとつ　128えんです。

　　A：これは？

　　B：それは　180えんです。

　　A：じゃ、これを　ください。

II A：すみません。62えんの　きってを　20まい　ください。

　　B：はい、どうぞ。

　　A：それから　41えんの　きってを　15まい　ください。いくらですか。

　　B：1,855えんです。

III A：いらっしゃいませ。

　　B：あの　かさを　みせて　ください。

　　A：どれですか。

　　B：あの　あおい　かさです。

　　A：これですか。どうぞ。

　　B：その　ちいさい　かさは　いくらですか。

　　A：これは　3,000えんです。

　　B：じゃ、この　かさを　ください。

I A. **Kono denchi wa ikura desu ka.** (How much is this battery?)
 B. **Sore wa hitotsu hyakunijūhachi-en desu.** (One of those is ¥128.)
 A. **Kore wa ?** (How about this one?)
 B. **Sore wa hyakuhachijū-en desu.** (That one is ¥180.)
 A. **Ja, kore o kudasai.** (Well, give me this one then.)

II A. **Sumimasen. Rokujūni-en no kitte o nijū-mai kudasai.** (Excuse me. I'd like twenty ¥62 postage stamps.)
 B. **Hai, dōzo.** (Here you are.)
 A. **Sorekara yonjūichi-en no kitte o jūgo-mai kudasai.** (Then I'd like fifteen ¥41 postage stamps, please.)
 　Ikura desu ka. (How much does that come to?)
 B. **Senhappyakugojūgo-en desu.** (That's ¥1,855.)

III A. **Irasshaimase.** (May I help you?)
 B. **Ano kasa o misete kudasai.** (Please show me that umbrella./I'd like to see that umbrella.)
 A. **Dore desu ka.** (Which one?)
 B. **Ano aoi kasa desu.** (The blue umbrella.)
 A. **Kore desu ka. Dōzo.** (This one? Here you are.)
 B. **Sono chiisai kasa wa ikura desu ka.** (How much is that small umbrella?)
 A. **Kore wa sanzen-en desu.** (This is ¥3,000.)
 B. **Ja, kono kasa o kudasai.** (I'll take this umbrella then.)

LESSON 6

Reading

STRUCTURE ～へ／に～ます。　～へ／に～ました。

1. わたしは あさって たいしかん<u>へ</u> いき<u>ます</u>。

2. むらたさんは きのうの ばん 9じに うち<u>に</u> かえり<u>ました</u>。

3. はやしさんの ともだちは あした にほん<u>へ</u> <u>き</u><u>ます</u>。

4. わたしたちは しゅうまつに きょうと<u>に</u> いき<u>ます</u>。

5. はやしさんの おくさんは せんしゅうの どようびに なりた くうこう<u>へ</u> いき<u>ました</u>。

6. もう 10じですから へや<u>へ</u> かえり<u>ます</u>。

7. せきぐちさんは きょねん おおさかから とうきょう<u>に</u> き<u>ました</u>。

Note that both *ni* and *e* can be used to indicate the direction of movement. The particle *e* is written へ.

Writing

Watashi wa asatte taishikan e ikimasu.

Mō jū-ji desu kara, heya e kaerimasu.

---

1. **Watashi wa asatte taishikan e ikimasu.** (I'm going to the embassy the day after tomorrow.)
2. **Murata-san wa kinō no ban ku-ji ni uchi ni kaerimashita.** (Mr. Murata went home at nine last night.)
3. **Hayashi-san no tomodachi wa ashita Nihon e kimasu.** (Mr. Hayashi's friend is coming to Japan tomorrow.)
4. **Watashi-tachi wa shūmatsu ni Kyōto ni ikimasu.** (We are going to Kyoto over the weekend.)
5. **Hayashi-san no okusan wa senshū no do-yōbi ni Narita Kūkō e ikimashita.** (Mr. Hayashi's wife went to Narita airport last Saturday.)
6. **Mō jū-ji desukara heya e kaerimasu.** (It's already 10 o'clock, so I'm going back to my room.)
7. **Sekiguchi-san wa kyonen Ōsaka kara Tōkyō ni kimashita.** (Mr. Sekiguchi came to Tokyo from Osaka last year.)

Hayashi-san no tomodachi wa ashita Nihon e kimasu.

Reading

I　A：いまから　よこはまへ　いきます。

　　B：かいしゃへ　かえりますか。

　　A：いいえ、かえりません。

II　A：こんにちは。よく　いらっしゃいました。どうぞ　こちらへ。

　　B：しつれいします。

　　A：どうぞ　おかけ　ください。

III　A：なつやすみに　どこへ　いきますか。

　　B：ともだちと　きゅうしゅうへ　いきます。

　　A：ひろしまにも　いきますか。

　　B：いいえ、ひろしまには　いきません。

I　A. **Ima kara Yokohama e ikimasu.** (I'm going to Yokohama right now.)
　　B. **Kaisha e kaerimasu ka.** (Will you return to the office?)
　　A. **Iie, kaerimasen.** (No, I won't.)
II　A. **Konnichiwa. Yoku irasshaimashita.** (Hello [welcome]!)
　　　Dōzo kochira e. (Please come in.)
　　B. **Shitsurei shimasu.** (May I [come in]?)
　　A. **Dōzo okake kudasai.** (Yes, please have a seat.)
III　A. **Natsu-yasumi ni doko e ikimasu ka.** (Where will you go for your summer vacation?)
　　B. **Tomodachi to Kyūshū e ikimasu.** (I'm going to Kyushu with a friend.)
　　A. **Hiroshima ni mo ikimasu ka.** (Will you be going to Hiroshima, too?)
　　B. **Iie, Hiroshima ni wa ikimasen.** (No, I won't [be going to Hiroshima].)

LESSON 7

Reading

STRUCTURE	〜は〜でした。 〜は〜では　ありませんでした。

1. かねださん**は** とうきょうでんきの べんごし**でした**。

2. おととい**は** わたしの たんじょうび**でした**。

3. きのう**は** やすみ**では ありませんでした**。

4. きのう**は** どようび**では ありませんでした**。

Writing

Ototoi wa watashi no tanjōbi deshita.

Kinō wa yasumi dewa arimasen deshita.

---

1. **Kaneda-san wa Tōkyō Denki no bengoshi deshita.** (Mr. Kaneda was a lawyer at Tokyo Electric.)
2. **Ototoi wa watashi no tanjōbi deshita.** (The day before yesterday was my birthday.)
3. **Kinō wa yasumi dewa arimasen deshita.** (Yesterday was not a holiday.)
4. **Kinō wa do-yōbi dewa arimasen deshita.** (Yesterday was not Saturday.)

Kaneda-san wa Tōkyō Denki no bengoshi deshita.

Reading

1. せんしゅう ぎんざで この かさを かいました。
   とけいも かいました。かさは 8,500えんでした。
   とけいは 39,000えんでした。

2. きのうは どようびでした。しごとは 12じまででした。
   きのうは ともだちの たんじょうびでした。ともだちと
   ばんごはんを たべました。そしてえいがを みました。

---

1. **Senshū Ginza de kono kasa o kaimashita. Tokei mo kaimashita. Kasa wa hassengohyaku-en deshita. Tokei wa sanmankyūsen-en deshita.**
   (I bought this umbrella in Ginza last week. I bought a watch, too. The umbrella was ¥8,500. The watch was ¥39,000.)
2. **Kinō wa do-yōbi deshita. Shigoto wa jūni-ji made deshita. Kinō wa tomodachi no tanjōbi deshita. Tomodachi to ban-gohan o tabemashita. Soshite eiga o mimashita.**
   (Yesterday was Saturday. I worked until 12:00. Yesterday was my friend's birthday. I had dinner with him/her. Then we saw a movie.)

LESSON 8

Reading and Writing

Write the following sentences vertically in the squares. The punctuation mark 。 is written in the upper right-hand quadrant of the square.

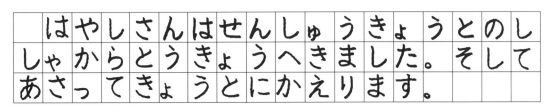

は	や	し	さ	ん	は	せ	ん	しゅ	う	きょ	う	と	の	し
しゃ	か	ら	と	う	きょ	う	へ	き	ま	し	た	。	そ	し	て
あ	さ	っ	て	きょ	う	と	に	か	え	り	ま	す	。		

Hayashi-san wa senshū Kyōto no shisha kara Tōkyō e kimashita. Soshite asatte Kyōto ni kaerimasu.

(Mr. Hayashi came to Tokyo from the branch office in Kyoto last week. He is going back to Kyoto the day after tomorrow.)

Reading and Writing

Write the following sentences vertically in the squares.

いまにかわむらさんとおくさんがいま
す。しょくどうにおとこのことおんなの
こがいます。だいどころにはだれもいま
せん。

いまにかわむらさんとおくさん
がいます。しょくどうにおとこの
ことおんなのこがいます。だいど
ころにはだれもいません。

KATAKANA

Katakana in Daily Life

Katakana is used in the following ways:

1. For words of foreign origin
2. For onomatopoeia

    e.g.: ワン　ワン (*wan wan*)＝bowbow

        ニャー　ニャー (*nyā nyā*)＝meow

        コケコッコー (*kokekokkō*)＝cock-a-doodle-doo

3. For emphasis

Katakana Chart

ア	イ	ウ	エ	オ
あ	い	う	え	お
a	i	u	e	o

カ	キ	ク	ケ	コ		ガ	ギ	グ	ゲ	ゴ
か	き	く	け	こ		が	ぎ	ぐ	げ	ご
ka	ki	ku	ke	ko		ga	gi	gu	ge	go
サ	シ	ス	セ	ソ		ザ	ジ	ズ	ゼ	ゾ
さ	し	す	せ	そ		ざ	じ	ず	ぜ	ぞ
sa	shi	su	se	so		za	ji	zu	ze	zo
タ	チ	ツ	テ	ト		ダ	ヂ	ヅ	デ	ド
た	ち	つ	て	と		だ	ぢ	づ	で	ど
ta	chi	tsu	te	to		da	ji	zu	de	do
ナ	ニ	ヌ	ネ	ノ						
な	に	ぬ	ね	の						
na	ni	nu	ne	no						
ハ	ヒ	フ	ヘ	ホ		バ	ビ	ブ	ベ	ボ
は	ひ	ふ	へ	ほ		ば	び	ぶ	べ	ぼ
ha	hi	fu	he	ho		ba	bi	bu	be	bo
マ	ミ	ム	メ	モ		パ	ピ	プ	ペ	ポ
ま	み	む	め	も		ぱ	ぴ	ぷ	ぺ	ぽ
ma	mi	mu	me	mo		pa	pi	pu	pe	po
ヤ		ユ		ヨ						
や		ゆ		よ						
ya		yu		yo						
ラ	リ	ル	レ	ロ						
ら	り	る	れ	ろ						
ra	ri	ru	re	ro						
ワ				ヲ						
わ				を						
wa				o						
ン										
ん										
n										

BASIC SYLLABLES

Writing

The gray lines are aids to accurate style. As with hiragana, in writing katakana, the stroke order is, as a rule, first from top to bottom, then from left to right.

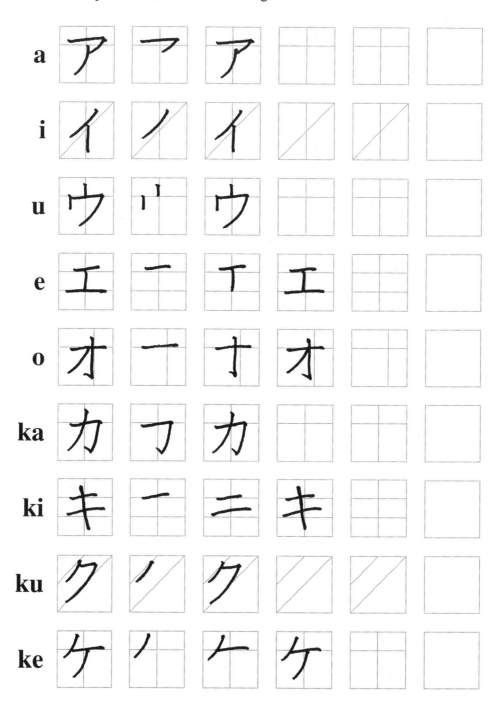

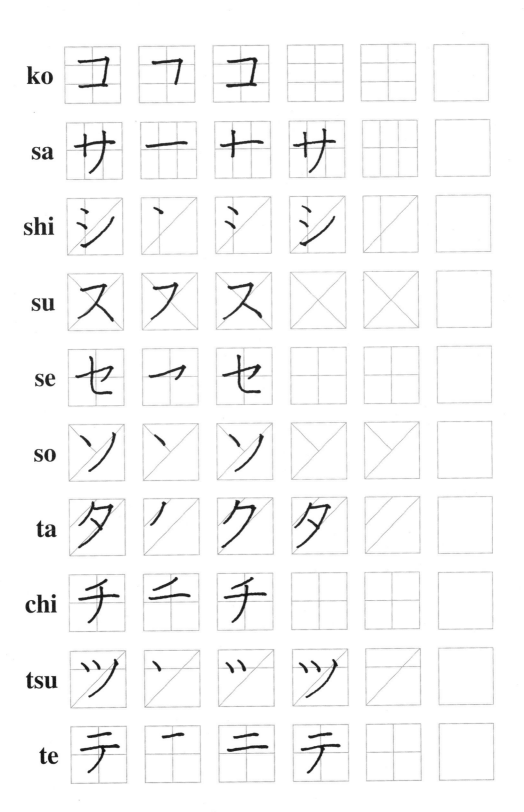

ko	ユ	フ	ユ			
sa	サ	十	サ			
shi	シ	ヽ	ミ	シ		
su	ス	フ	ス			
se	セ	マ	セ			
so	ソ	ヽ	ソ			
ta	タ	ノ	ク	タ		
chi	チ	二	チ			
tsu	ツ	ヽ	ツ	ツ		
te	テ	ニ	ニ	テ		

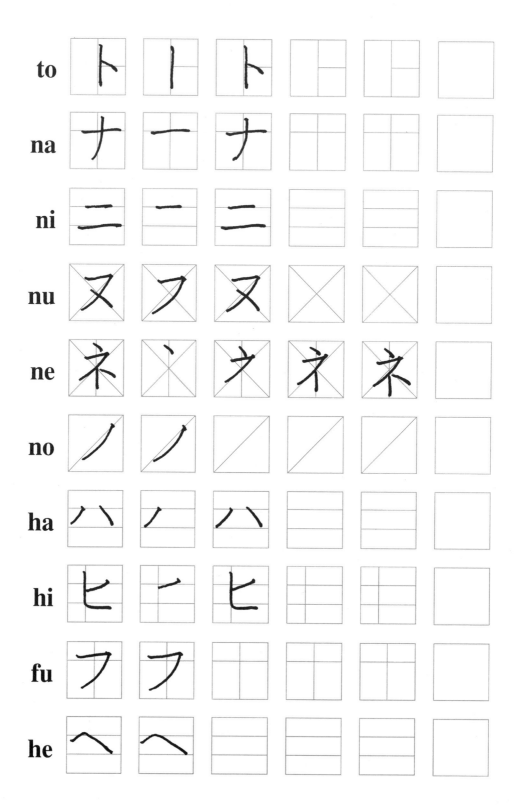

to	ト	｜	ト		
na	ナ	一	ナ		
ni	二	一	二		
nu	ヌ	ヌ	ヌ		
ne	ネ	丶	ヌ	ネ	ネ
no	ノ	ノ			
ha	ハ	ノ	ハ		
hi	ヒ	一	ヒ		
fu	フ	フ			
he	ヘ	ヘ			

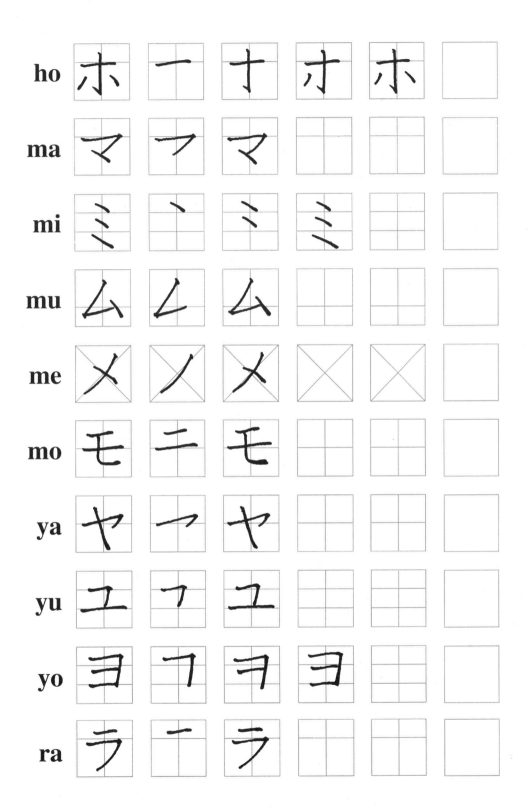

ho	ホ	一	十	オ	ホ	
ma	マ	フ	マ			
mi	ミ	ヽ	ミ	ミ		
mu	ム	ム	ム			
me	メ	ノ	メ			
mo	モ	二	モ			
ya	ヤ	一	ヤ			
yu	ユ	フ	ユ			
yo	ヨ	ラ	ヲ	ヨ		
ra	ラ	一	ラ			

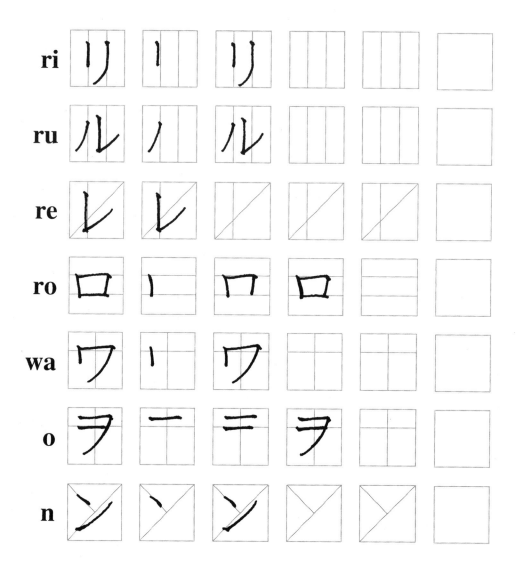

ri	リ		リ			
ru	ル	ノ	ル			
re	レ	レ				
ro	ロ	ロ	ロ			
wa	ワ	ワ				
o	ヲ	二	ヲ			
n	ン	ン	ン			

Reading and Writing

The following look-alike *katakana* are easily confused. Read and write them.

シ ツ **shi tsu** ☐☐   ク タ **ku ta** ☐☐

ウ ワ **u wa** ☐☐   ヒ エ **hi e** ☐☐

サ ナ **sa na** ☐☐   マ ム **ma mu** ☐☐

ア ム **a mu** ☐☐   オ ホ **o ho** ☐☐

ワ フ **wa fu** ☐☐   ヌ ス **nu su** ☐☐

ニ ミ **ni mi** ☐☐   メ ナ **me na** ☐☐

ノ ハ **no ha** ☐☐   ル レ **ru re** ☐☐

イ ト **i to** ☐☐   ソ ン **so n** ☐☐

チ テ **chi te** ☐☐   ヨ コ **yo ko** ☐☐

MODIFIED SYLLABLES

Reading and Writing

1. Modified syllables (e.g., *kya, kyu, kyo*) and double consonants are written in *katakana* in the same way as in *hiragana*.

1. キャベツ 2. キャスト 3. ギリシャ

4. シャンペン 5. ジャスト 6. ショック

7. キッチン 8. コップ 9. ショッピング

---

1. **kyabetsu** (cabbage) 2. **kyasuto** (cast) 3. **Girisha** (Greece)
4. **shampen** (champagne) 5. **jasuto** (just) 6. **shokku** (shock)
7. **kitchin** (kitchen) 8. **koppu** (cup) 9. **shoppingu** (shopping)

2. Long sounds are represented by a dash, ー.

10. ビール 11. ボール 12. コーヒー

13. スキー 14. デパート 15. スープ

---

10. **bīru** (beer) 11. **bōru** (ball) 12. **kōhī** (coffee)
13. **sukī** (ski) 14. **depāto** (department store) 15. **sūpu** (soup)

3. Some syllables (sounds), such as English "di," "ti," "fa," do not exist in the Japanese syllabary and therefore can't be transliterated directly into *katakana*. They are represented by such combinations as seen in the following examples.

16. デュエット 17. デューク 18. ディスコ

19. ファイト 20. フェンス 21. フィールド

22. フォーク 23. ヴァイオリン

24. ヴィーナス 25. ヴェニス 26. スウェーデン

27. パーティー 28. テューター 29. クォーツ

30. クォリティー

---

16. **duetto** (duet) 17. **dūku** (duke) 18. **disuko** (disco)
19. **faito** (fight) 20. **fensu** (fence) 21. **fīrudo** (field)
22. **fōku** (folk) 23. **vaiorin** (violin)
24. **Vīnasu** (Venus) 25. **Venisu** (Venice) 26. **Suēden** (Sweden)
27. **pātī** (party) 28. **tyūtā** (tutor) 29. **kuōtsu** (quartz)
30. **kuoritī** (quality)

Reading and Writing

First read the words in *katakana*, covering the romanization. Then write them, covering the *katakana*.

1. アメリカ   **Amerika**

2. イギリス   **Igirisu**

3. フランス   **Furansu**

4. ドイツ   **Doitsu**

5. ニューヨーク **Nyūyōku**

6. ロンドン   **Rondon**

7. スミス   **Sumisu**

8. ホワイト   **Howaito**

9. ブラウン   **Buraun**

---

1. America   2. England   3. France
4. Germany   5. New York   6. London
7. Smith   8. White   9. Brown

Reading and Writing

1. カメラ   **kamera**   ☐☐☐

2. テレビ   **terebi**   ☐☐☐

3. ラジオ   **rajio**   ☐☐☐

4. バス   **basu**   ☐☐

5. キロ   **kiro**   ☐☐

6. グラム   **guramu**   ☐☐☐

7. ビル   **biru**   ☐☐

8. パン   **pan**   ☐☐

9. デパート   **depāto**   ☐☐☐☐

10. スーパー   **sūpā**   ☐☐☐☐

---

1. camera   2. television   3. radio   4. bus
5. kilo   6. gram   7. building   8. bread
9. department store   10. supermarket

Reading and Writing

The following words are from the illustration on p. 68, 69. First read the words in *katakana*, covering the romanization. Then write them, covering the *katakana*.

1. サラダ   **sarada**

2. コーラ   **kōra**

3. ピザ   **piza**

4. チーズ   **chīzu**

5. バナナ   **banana**

6. チョコレート   **chokorēto**

7. スカート   **sukāto**

8. ズボン   **zubon**

9. ネクタイ   **nekutai**

10. ジャケット   **jaketto**

---

1. salad   2. cola   3. pizza   4. cheese   5. banana
6. chocolate   7. skirt   8. trousers   9. necktie
10. suit jacket

TEST YOUR READING ABILITY 1

4 パイプ
6 スカーフ
3 セーター
8 ソファー
5 コーヒー
2 タバコ
7 スカート
12 ソーセージ
9 ウィスキー
11 ブランデー
14 ハム
27 ピザ
15 チーズ
20 メロン
16 サラダ
22 コーラ
17 パイナップル
21 オレンジ
18 バナナ
23 テーブルクロス

1 シャンデリア

29 イヤリング

28 ピアノ

30 ワイシャツ

32 ネクタイ

1 ネックレス

34 カクテル

10 ワイン

13 グラス

35 ベルト

33 ジャケット

36 スーツ

38 バッグ

19 ビール

37 ワンピース

24 ナイフ

25 フォーク

26 スプーン

39 ズボン

40 ハイヒール

TEST YOUR READING ABILITY 2

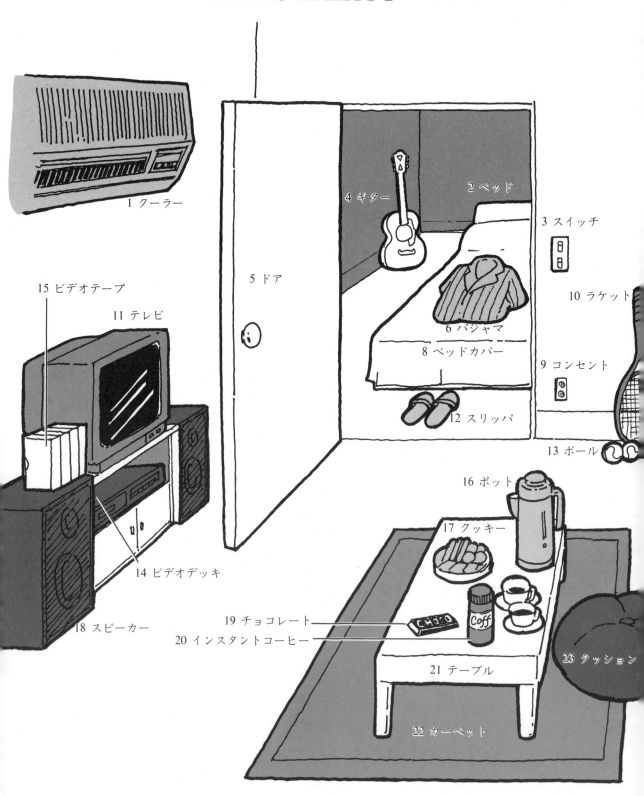

1 クーラー

4 ギター

2 ベッド

3 スイッチ

15 ビデオテープ

11 テレビ

5 ドア

10 ラケット

6 パジャマ

8 ベッドカバー

9 コンセント

12 スリッパ

13 ボール

14 ビデオデッキ

16 ポット

17 クッキー

18 スピーカー

19 チョコレート

20 インスタントコーヒー

21 テーブル

23 クッション

22 カーペット

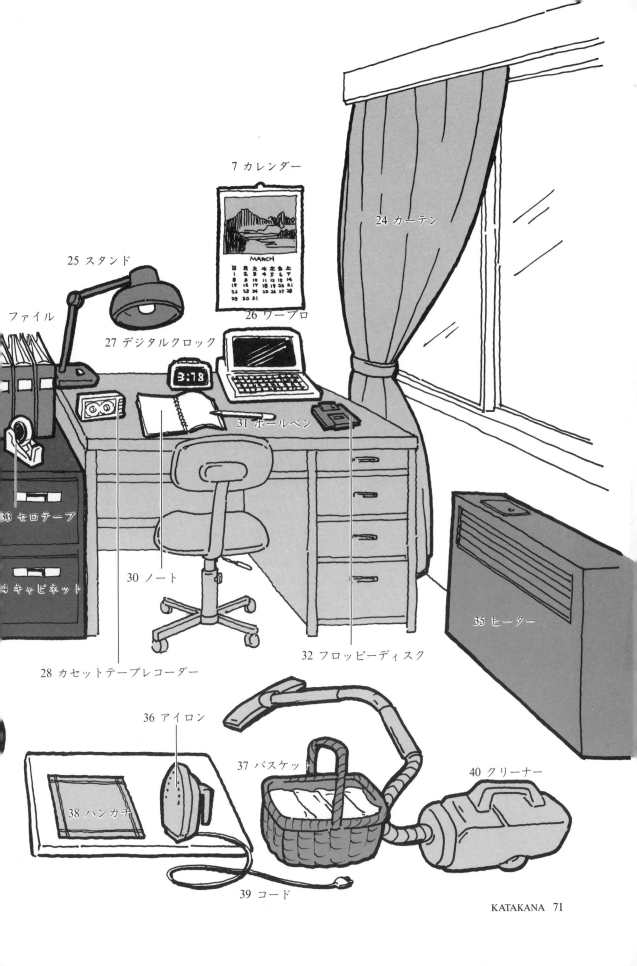

7 カレンダー

24 カーテン

25 スタンド

ファイル

27 デジタルクロック

26 ワープロ

33 セロテープ

31 ボールペン

4 キャビネット

30 ノート

35 ヒーター

32 フロッピーディスク

28 カセットテープレコーダー

36 アイロン

37 バスケット

40 クリーナー

38 ハンカチ

39 コード

1	shanderia	chandelier
2	tabako	cigarette
3	sētā	sweater
4	paipu	pipe
5	kōhī	coffee
6	sukāfu	scarf
7	sukāto	skirt
8	sofā	sofa
9	uisukī	whisky
10	wain	wine
11	burandē	brandy
12	sōsēji	sausage
13	gurasu	drinking glass
14	hamu	ham
15	chīzu	cheese
16	sarada	salad
17	painappuru	pineapple
18	banana	banana
19	bīru	beer
20	meron	melon
21	orenji	orange
22	kōra	cola
23	tēburukurosu	tablecloth
24	naifu	knife
25	fōku	fork
26	supūn	spoon
27	piza	pizza
28	piano	piano
29	iyaringu	earring
30	waishatsu	dress shirt
31	nekkuresu	necklace
32	nekutai	necktie
33	jaketto	suit jacket
34	kakuteru	cocktail
35	beruto	belt
36	sūtsu	suit
37	wanpīsu	a dress
38	baggu	purse
39	zubon	trousers
40	haihīru	high-heeled shoes

1	kūrā	cooler, air conditioner
2	beddo	bed
3	suitchi	switch
4	gitā	guitar
5	doa	door
6	pajama	pajamas
7	karendā	calendar
8	beddokabā	bedspread
9	konsento	wall socket/outlet
10	raketto	racket
11	terebi	television
12	surippa	slippers
13	bōru	ball
14	bideodekki	video deck
15	bideotēpu	videotapes
16	potto	thermos jug
17	kukkī	cookies
18	supīkā	speaker
19	chokorēto	chocolate
20	insutantokōhī	instant coffee
21	tēburu	table
22	kāpetto	carpet
23	kusshon	cushion
24	kāten	curtain
25	sutando	desk lamp
26	wāpuro	word processor
27	dejitarukurokku	digital clock
28	kasettotēpurekōdā	cassette tape recorder
29	fairu	file
30	nōto	notebook
31	bōrupen	ball-point pen
32	furoppīdisuku	floppy disk
33	serotēpu	scotch tape
34	kyabinetto	cabinet
35	hītā	heater
36	airon	iron
37	basuketto	basket
38	hankachi	handkerchief
39	kōdo	code
40	kurīnā	vacuum cleaner

TEST YOUR WRITING ABILITY

Try writing the following English words in *katakana*, following the examples.

jam→ ジ ャ ム   hotel→ ホ テ ル

sport(s)→ ス ポ ー ツ   test→ テ ス ト

lunch→ ラ ン チ   match→ マ ッ チ

super→ ス ー パ ー   top→ ト ッ プ

soup→ ス ー プ   party→ パ ー テ ィ ー

1. tennis→ ☐ ☐ ☐   2. golf→ ☐ ☐ ☐

3. milk→ ☐ ☐ ☐

4. concert→ ☐ ☐ ☐ ☐   5. box→ ☐ ☐ ☐ ☐

6. maker→ ☐ ☐ ☐ ☐   7. user→ ☐ ☐ ☐ ☐

8. system→ ☐ ☐ ☐ ☐   9. money→ ☐ ☐ ☐

10. schedule→ ☐ ☐ ☐ ☐ ☐ ☐

11. computer→ ☐ ☐ ☐ ☐ ☐ ☐ ☐

---

1. テニス   2. ゴルフ   3. ミルク   4. コンサート   5. ボックス
   tenisu   gorufu   miruku   konsāto   bokkusu

6. メーカー   7. ユーザー   8. システム   9. マネー
   mēkā   yūzā   shisutemu   manē

10. スケジュール   11. コンピューター
    sukejūru   kompūtā

TEST YOUR WRITING ABILITY

coat, court → | コ | ー | ト |

bath, bus → | バ | ス |

food, hood → | フ | ー | ド |

light, right → | ラ | イ | ト |

1. lighter, writer → | | | | |

2. leader, reader → | | | | |

3. hall, hole → | | | |

4. sauce, source → | | | |

5. loan, lawn → | | | |

6. ball, bowl → | | | |

---

1. ライター   2. リーダー   3. ホール   4. ソース
   raitā   rīdā   hōru   sōsu

5. ローン   6. ボール
   rōn   bōru

READING REVIEW

READING REVIEW

1　きのう バスで ぎんざへ いきました。デパートで レコードを かいました。きっさてんで ジュースを のみました。そして タクシーで うちに かえりました。

1. **Kinō basu de Ginza e ikimashita. Depāto de rekōdo o kaimashita. Kissaten de jūsu o nomimashita. Soshite takushī de uchi ni kaerimashita.**

   I went to Ginza by bus yesterday. I bought a record in a department store. I had some juice in a coffee shop. Then I went home by taxi.

2. **Sumisu-san wa sengetsu Amerika kara Nihon e kimashita. Ashita okusan ga kimasu. Raigetsu okusan to Igirisu ni ikimasu.**

   Mr. Smith came to Japan from America last month. His wife is coming tomorrow. He is going to England with her next month.

3. **Ima ni ōkii terebi ga arimasu. Tsukue no ue ni tēpurekōdā ga arimasu. Daidokoro ni rajio ga arimasu.**

   There is a big television in the living room. There is a tape recorder on the desk. There is a radio in the kitchen.

2　スミスさんは せんげつ アメリカから にほんへ きました。あした おくさんが きます。らいげつ おくさんと イギリスに いきます。

3　いまに おおきい テレビが あります。つくえの うえに テープレコーダーが あります。だいどころに ラジオが あります。

4

きのうはやすみでした。あさからとてもいいてんきでしたから、ともだちとテニスをしました。ドイツたいしかんのちかくにテニスコートがあります。くるまでテニスコートまでいきました。うちからテニスコートまでくるまで15ふんぐらいです。11じごろうちへかえりました。

ともだちもうちにきました。うちでシャワーをあびました。そしてジュースをのみました。ひる ふたりでサンドイッチをたべました。それからビールものみました。

ごご ぎんざでフランスのえいがをみました。 とてもロマンチックなえいがでした。そのあとデパートでかいものをしました。あしたはしゅじんのたんじょうびですから、ネクタイをかいました。それからシャンペンもかいました。

Vocabulary

テニスコート **tenisukōto** (tennis court)　シャワーをあびます **shawā o abimasu** (take a shower)

ロマンチック **romanchikku** (romantic)　そのあと **sono ato** (after that)

Kinō wa yasumi deshita. Asa kara totemo ii tenki deshita kara, tomodachi to tenisu o shimashita. Doitsu taishikan no chikaku ni tenisukōto ga arimasu. Kuruma de tenisukōto made ikimashita. Uchi kara tenisukōto made kuruma de jūgo-fun gurai desu. Jūichi-ji goro uchi e kaerimashita.

Tomodachi mo uchi ni kimashita. Uchi de shawā o abimashita. Soshite jūsu o nomimashita. Hiru futari de sandoitchi o tabemashita. Sorekara bīru mo nomimashita.

Gogo Ginza de Furansu no eiga o mimashita. Totemo romanchikku na eiga deshita. Sono ato depāto de kaimono o shimashita. Ashita wa shujin no tanjōbi desu kara, nekutai o kaimashita. Sorekara shampen mo kaimashita.

Yesterday was a holiday. It was very fine from morning, so I played tennis with a friend. There is a tennis court near the German embassy. We went to the tennis court by car. It takes about fifteen minutes from my house to the court by car. I got home about 11:00.

My friend came home with me. We took a shower. Then we had some juice. We had sandwitches together for lunch. We also had some beer.

We saw a French movie in Ginza in the afternoon. It was a very romantic movie. After that, we did some shopping in a department store. Tomorrow is my husband's birthday, so I bought a necktie. And then I bought some champagne, too.

コミュニケーションのための日本語　かなワークブック
JAPANESE FOR BUSY PEOPLE　Kana Workbook

1996年 6 月　第 1 刷発行
2002年 1 月　第 7 刷発行

著　者　社団法人　国際日本語普及協会

発行者　野間佐和子

発行所　講談社インターナショナル株式会社
　　　　〒112-8652 東京都文京区音羽 1-17-14
　　　　電話　03-3944-6493（編集部）
　　　　　　　03-3944-6492（営業部・業務部）
　　　　ホームページ　http://www.kodansha-intl.co.jp

印刷所　大日本印刷株式会社

製本所　大日本印刷株式会社

KODANSHA INTERNATIONAL DICTIONARIES
Easy-to-use dictionaries designed for non-native learners of Japanese.

KODANSHA'S FURIGANA JAPANESE DICTIONARY
JAPANESE-ENGLISH / ENGLISH-JAPANESE ふりがな和英・英和辞典

Both of Kodansha's popular furigana dictionaries in one portable, affordable volume. A truly comprehensive and practical dictionary for English-speaking learners, and an invaluable guide to using the Japanese language.
- Basic vocabulary of 30,000 entries
- Hundreds of special words, names, and phrases
- Clear explanations of semantic and usage differences
- Special information on grammar and usage

Hardcover, 1318 pages, ISBN 4-7700-2480-0

KODANSHA'S FURIGANA JAPANESE-ENGLISH DICTIONARY
新装版 ふりがな和英辞典

The essential dictionary for all students of Japanese.
- Furigana readings added to all *kanji*
- Comprehensive 16,000-word basic vocabulary

Paperback, 592 pages, ISBN 4-7700-2750-8

KODANSHA'S FURIGANA ENGLISH-JAPANESE DICTIONARY
新装版 ふりがな英和辞典

The companion to the essential dictionary for all students of Japanese.
- Furigana readings added to all *kanji*
- Comprehensive 14,000-word basic vocabulary

Paperback, 728 pages, ISBN 4-7700-2751-6

KODANSHA'S CONCISE ROMANIZED JAPANESE-ENGLISH DICTIONARY
コンサイス版 ローマ字和英辞典

A first, basic dictionary for beginner students of Japanese.
- Comprehensive 10,000-word basic vocabulary
- Easy-to-find romanized entries listed in alphabetical order
- Definitions written for English-speaking users
- Sample sentences in romanized and standard Japanese script, followed by the English translation

Paperback, 480 pages, ISBN 4-7700-2849-0

KODANSHA'S ROMANIZED JAPANESE-ENGLISH DICTIONARY
新装版 ローマ字和英辞典

A portable reference written for beginning and intermediate students.
- 16,000-word vocabulary
- No knowledge of *kanji* necessary

Paperback, 688 pages, ISBN 4-7700-2753-2

KODANSHA'S BASIC ENGLISH-JAPANESE DICTIONARY
日常日本語バイリンガル辞典

An annotated dictionary useful for both students and teachers.
- Over 4,500 entries and 18,000 vocabulary items
- Examples and information on stylistic differences
- Appendixes for technical terms, syntax and grammar

Vinyl flexibinding, 1520 pages, ISBN 4-7700-2628-5

THE MODERN ENGLISH-NIHONGO DICTIONARY
日本語学習英日辞典

The first truly bilingual dictionary designed exclusively for non-native learners of Japanese.
- Over 6,000 headwords
- Both standard Japanese with *furigana* and romanized orthography
- Sample sentences provided for most entries
- Numerous explanatory notes and *kanji* guides

Vinyl flexibinding, 1200 pages, ISBN 4-7700-2148-8

KODANSHA'S ELEMENTARY KANJI DICTIONARY

新装版 教育漢英熟語辞典

A first, basic *kanji* dictionary for non-native learners of Japanese.
• Complete guide to 1,006 *Shin-kyōiku kanji* • Over 10,000 common compounds
• Three indices for finding *kanji* • Compact, portable format • Functional, up-to-date, timely
Paperback, 576 pages, ISBN 4-7700-2752-4

KODANSHA'S COMPACT KANJI GUIDE

常用漢英熟語辞典

A functional character dictionary that is both compact and comprehensive.
• 1,945 essential *jōyō kanji* • 20,000 common compounds • Three indexes for finding *kanji*
Vinyl flexibinding, 928 pages, ISBN 4-7700-1553-4

THE KODANSHA KANJI LEARNER'S DICTIONARY

新装版 漢英学習字典

The perfect kanji tool for beginners to advanced learners.
• Revolutionary SKIP lookup method • Five lookup methods and three indexes
• 2,230 entries & 41,000 meanings for 31,000 words
Paperback, 1060 pages (2-color), ISBN 4-7700-2855-5

KODANSHA'S EFFECTIVE JAPANESE USAGE DICTIONARY

新装版 日本語使い分け辞典

A concise, bilingual dictionary which clarifies the usage of frequently confused words and phrases.
• Explanations of 708 synonymous terms • Numerous example sentences
Paperback, 768 pages, ISBN 4-7700-2850-4

A DICTIONARY OF JAPANESE PARTICLES

てにをは辞典

Treats over 100 particles in alphabetical order, providing sample sentences for each meaning.
• Meets students' needs from beginning to advanced levels
• Treats principal particle meanings as well as variants
Paperback, 368 pages, ISBN 4-7700-2352-9

THE HANDBOOK OF JAPANESE VERBS

日本語動詞ハンドブック *Taeko Kamiya*

An indispensable reference and guide to Japanese verbs aimed at beginning and intermediate students. Precisely the book that verb-challenged students have been looking for.
• Verbs are grouped, conjugated, and combined with auxiliaries
• Different forms are used in sentences
• Each form is followed by reinforcing examples and exercises
Paperback, 256pages, ISBN 4-7700-2683-8

A DICTIONARY OF BASIC JAPANESE SENTENCE PATTERNS

日本語基本文型辞典

Author of the best-selling All About Particles explains fifty of the most common, basic patterns and their variations, along with numerous contextual examples. Both a reference and a textbook for students at all levels.
• Formulas delineating basic pattern structure • Commentary on individual usages
Paperback, 320 pages, ISBN 4-7700-2608-0

HIRAGANA・KATAKANA CHART

あ ア a	い イ i	う ウ u	え エ e	お オ o
か カ ka	き キ ki	く ク ku	け ケ ke	こ コ ko
さ サ sa	し シ shi	す ス su	せ セ se	そ ソ so
た タ ta	ち チ chi	つ ツ tsu	て テ te	と ト to
な ナ na	に ニ ni	ぬ ヌ nu	ね ネ ne	の ノ no

が ガ ga	ぎ ギ gi	ぐ グ gu	げ ゲ ge	ご ゴ go
ざ ザ za	じ ジ ji	ず ズ zu	ぜ ゼ ze	ぞ ゾ zo
だ ダ da	ぢ ヂ ji	づ ヅ zu	で デ de	ど ド do